Caterpillars

by Helen Frost

Consulting Editor: Gail Saunders-Smith, Ph.D.

Consultant: Dr. Ronald L. Rutowski,
Professor of Biology, Arizona State University

Pebble Books

an imprint of Capstone Press
Mankato, Minnesota

Pebble Books are published by Capstone Press
151 Good Counsel Drive, P.O. Box 669, Mankato, Minnesota 56002
http://www.capstone-press.com

2 3 4 5 6 04 03 02 01 00

Library of Congress Cataloging-in-Publication Data
Frost, Helen, 1949–
    Caterpillars/by Helen Frost.
    p. cm.—(Butterflies)
    Includes bibliographical references and index.
    Summary: An introduction to the stages a caterpillar goes through as it
develops from egg to butterfly.
    ISBN 0-7368-0228-2
    1. Caterpillars—Juvenile literature. [1. Caterpillars.] I. Title. II. Series:
Frost, Helen, 1949– Butterflies.
QL544.2.F768 1999
595.78′139—dc21   98-44903
                                                           CIP
                                                           AC

Note to Parents and Teachers

The Butterflies series supports national science standards related to the diversity and unity of life. This book describes how caterpillars change and grow into butterflies. The species featured in this book is a black swallowtail. The photographs support early readers in understanding the text. The repetition of words and phrases helps early readers learn new words. This book also introduces early readers to subject-specific vocabulary words, which are defined in the Words to Know section. Early readers may need assistance to read some words and to use the Table of Contents, Words to Know, Read More, Internet Sites, and Index/Word List sections of the book.

Table of Contents

4

A caterpillar hatches
from an egg.

The caterpillar eats plants.

8

The caterpillar grows.

The caterpillar molts. It crawls out of its old skin.

12

The caterpillar eats
and grows.

The caterpillar molts again. It molts four or five times.

The caterpillar hangs
upside down.

18

The caterpillar becomes a chrysalis.

20

The chrysalis will become a butterfly.

Words to Know

butterfly—an insect with large, colored wings; butterflies live everywhere in the world except Antarctica.

caterpillar—the second life stage of a butterfly; caterpillars molt and become chrysalises.

chrysalis—the third life stage of a butterfly; adult butterflies come out of chrysalises.

egg—the first life stage of a butterfly; caterpillars hatch from eggs.

molt—to shed skin so that new skin can grow; caterpillars molt several times as they grow.

Read More

Facklam, Margery. *Creepy, Crawly Caterpillars.* Boston: Little, Brown and Company, 1996.

Ling, Mary. *Butterfly.* See How They Grow. New York: Dorling Kindersley, 1992.

Saunders-Smith, Gail. *Butterflies.* Animals: Life Cycles. Mankato, Minn.: Pebble Books, 1997.

Internet Sites

The Butterfly Website
http://butterflywebsite.com

Children's Butterfly Site
http://www.mesc.nbs.gov/butterfly/Butterfly.html

Where Do Butterflies Come From?
http://www.hhmi.org/coolscience/butterfly/
  index.html

Index/Word List

Word Count: 54
Early-Intervention Level: 9

Editorial Credits

Colleen Sexton, editor; Steve Christensen, cover designer; Kimberly Danger and Sheri Gosewisch, photo researchers

Photo Credits

Barrett and MacKay Photo, 1
Connie Toops, 16
Dwight R. Kuhn, cover
Fred Siskind, 4, 8, 14, 18, 20
Kate Boykin, 10
Visuals Unlimited/Dick Poe, 6; Leroy Simon, 12

24